DISNEP
LEARNING

Meet Elsa

ADVENTURES IN READING

Based on the story *A Sister More Like Me*
by Barbara Jean Hicks
Illustrated by Brittney Lee

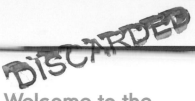

Welcome to the
Disney Learning Programme!

Sharing a book with your child is the perfect opportunity to cuddle and enjoy the reading experience together. Research has shown that reading aloud with your child is one of the most important ways to prepare them for success as a reader. When you share books with each other, you help strengthen your child's reading and vocabulary skills as well as stimulate their curiosity, imagination and enthusiasm for reading.

In this book meet Princess Elsa, and learn about her magical powers. Are they strong enough to keep her apart from her sister, Anna? You can enhance the reading experience by talking to your child about their own talents or abilities. What sort of things do they like doing? What are their special talents or gifts? Children find it easier to understand what they read when they can connect it with their own personal experiences.

Children learn in different ways and at different speeds, but they all require a supportive environment to nurture a lifelong love of books, reading and learning. The *Adventures in Reading* books are carefully levelled to present new challenges to developing readers. They are filled with familiar and fun characters from the wonderful world of Disney to make the learning experience comfortable, positive and enjoyable.

Enjoy your reading adventure together!

Scholastic Children's Books
Euston House,
24 Eversholt Street,
London NW1 1DB, UK

A division of Scholastic Ltd
London • New York • Toronto • Sydney • Auckland
Mexico City • New Delhi • Hong Kong

This book was first published in Australia in 2015 by Scholastic Australia.
This edition published in the UK by Scholastic Ltd in 2015.

ISBN 978 1 4071 6299 7

Printed in Malaysia

2 4 6 8 10 9 7 5 3 1

Papers used by Scholastic Children's Books are made from woods grown in sustainable forests.

www.scholastic.co.uk

Elsa is a young princess.
She is very clever. She
is quiet and graceful.

Elsa has a sister.
Her name is Anna.
Anna is Elsa's little sister.

When Elsa was little, her parents realised that she had special powers. Magic came from her hands. She could make things out of ice and snow.

Elsa's mum and dad were afraid.
They told her not to use her magic.
Elsa had to stay in her room,
away from her sister.

Anna wanted to play, but Elsa
always kept her door closed.
She did not want to hurt Anna.

Anna did not understand, so she learned to play alone. She dreamed of the day when she could play with Elsa again.

Sometimes, Elsa was lonely. Anna did not remember Elsa's magic, so Elsa had to keep it a secret.

Elsa worked hard to control her
power. She liked to study, too.
It was fun to read and write.

As Anna and Elsa grew older,
they became more and more different.
Elsa woke up early every morning.
She liked everything to be neat and tidy.

Anna slept in every morning.
Her bedroom was always messy.
She did not mind if things were untidy.

Elsa liked peace and quiet. She worried about hurting someone outside the castle with her magic. So she was happy to stay inside.

The two sisters were not unhappy.
But they missed the fun that they
once had together.

One day, Elsa left the castle.
She was tired of hiding her magic,
so she built an icy palace. When
Anna saw it, she was amazed!

The sisters realised that their love
was stronger than any magic!
They would not stay apart any longer.

Elsa no longer keeps her magic a secret. Now her little sister is her best friend, too.